RECORDED VERSIONS GUITAR

AUTHENTIC TRANSCRIPTIONS
WITH NOTES AND TABLATURE

DEATH CAB FOR CUTIE   NARROW STAIRS

Music transcriptions by Pete Billmann

ISBN 978-1-4234-6245-3

HAL•LEONARD® CORPORATION

7777 W. BLUEMOUND RD. P.O. BOX 13819 MILWAUKEE, WI 53213

In Australia Contact:
Hal Leonard Australia Pty. Ltd.
4 Lentara Court
Cheltenham, Victoria, 3192 Australia
Email: ausadmin@halleonard.com.au

Visit Hal Leonard Online at
www.halleonard.com

Bixby Canyon Bridge

Words and Music by Benjamin Gibbard

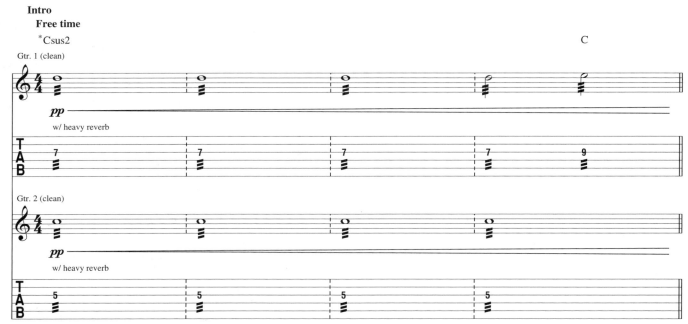

*Chord symbols reflect combined harmony.

And bare - foot   in _____   the shal - low creek, ___   I grabbed some   stones _____

from un - der - neath _____   and wait - ed for you _____   to speak _   to me. _

Verse

Gtrs. 1 & 2: w/ Riffs A & A1 (2 times)

Fmaj7

C

2. In the si - lence, __ it be-

End Riff B

End Riff B1

Gtr. 3 tacet

Am   C   Am   C

came so ver - y clear   that you had   long a - go dis - ap - peared. ____ I cursed my-

Gtr. 4 (clean)

pp ——— mp

w/ heavy reverb

Am   C   Am

self for be - ing sur - prised ____   that this did - n't play like it did   in my mind. __

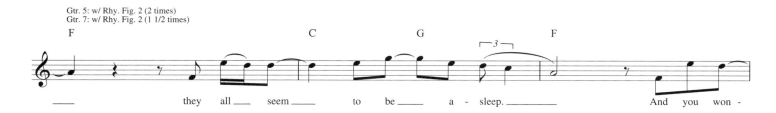

they all ___ seem ___ to be ___ a - sleep. ___ And you won -

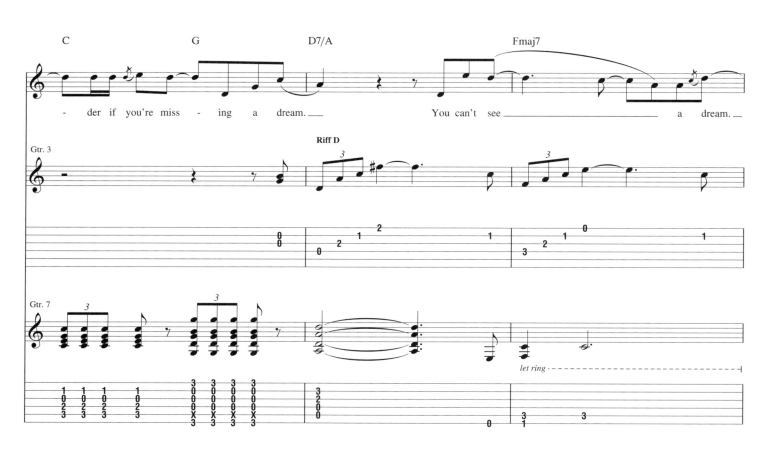

- der if you're miss - ing a dream. ___ You can't see ___ a dream. ___

Gtr. 3

Riff D

Gtr. 7

let ring -

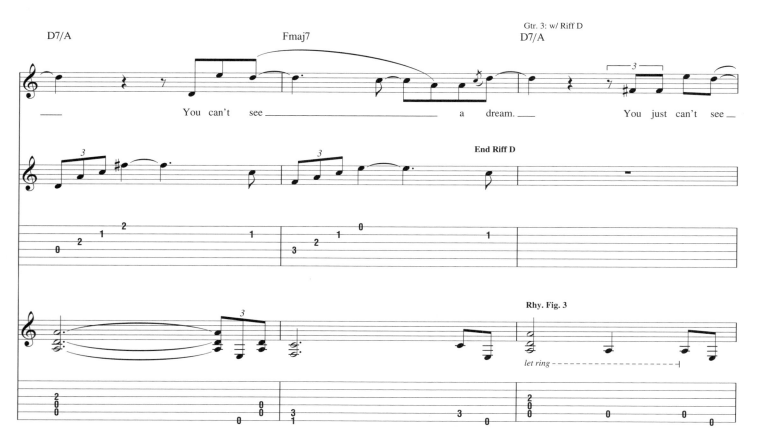

You can't see ___ a dream. ___ You just can't see ___

End Riff D

Rhy. Fig. 3

let ring -

Gtr. 8: w/ Riff E (2 times)

dream, _____ a dream, _____ a

Gtr. 9 (dist.)

f

dream. _____

Interlude

Gtrs. 7 & 9

*Chord symbols reflect implied harmony.

1., 2., 3.

w/ misc. fdbk. & delay effects (next 2 meas.)   Gtrs. 7 & 9 tacet

Outro

w/ misc. fdbk. & delay effects (next 8 meas.)

N.C.

And then it start-ed get-ting dark and I trudged back to where the car ___ was parked. ___

___ No clos-er to an-y kind __ of truth, as I must as-sume was the case __ with you. ___

I Will Possess Your Heart

Words and Music by Benjamin Gibbard, Jason McGerr, Nicholas Harmer and Christopher Walla

*Played behind the beat.

**Vol. swell

Gtr. 3

* w/ delay - - - - - - - - - - - - - - -

*Delay set for quarter-note triplet
regeneration w/ 5 repeats.

Gtr. 1: w/ Riff B

Gtr. 1: w/ Riff B

Gtr. 1: w/ Riff B

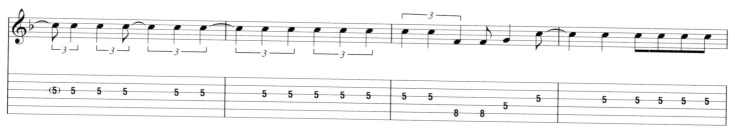

1. How I wish you could see the po-ten-tial, the po-ten-tial of you and me. ___

*Symbols in parentheses represent chord names respective to capoed guitar.
Symbols above reflect actual sounding chords. Capoed fret is "0" in tab.

It's like a book el-e-gant-ly bound,— but in a lan-guage that you can't read— just yet.

Chorus

You got-ta spend some time, love. You got-ta spend some time with me.

And I know that you'll find, love, I will pos-sess your heart. ___

You got-ta spend some time, love. You got-ta spend some time with me.

And I know that you'll find, love, I will pos-sess your heart. ___

Interlude

Verse

2. There are days when out-side your win-dow I see my re-flec-tion as I slow-ly pass. ___

And I long for this mir-rored per-spec-tive when we'll be lov-ers, lov-ers at last. ___

*Chord symbols reflect implied harmony.
**Refers to upstemmed voc. only.

20

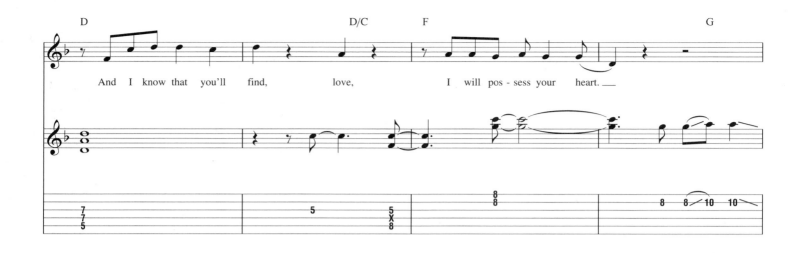

Bkgd. Voc.: w/ Voc. Fig. 2

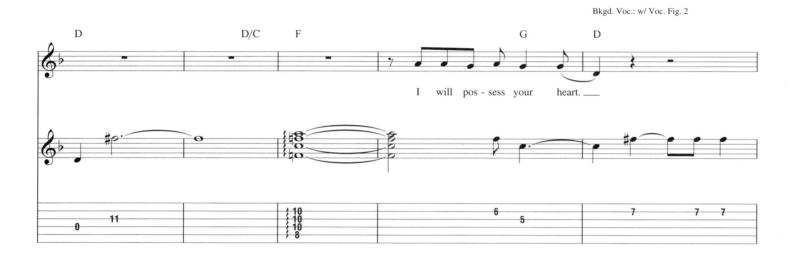

Outro

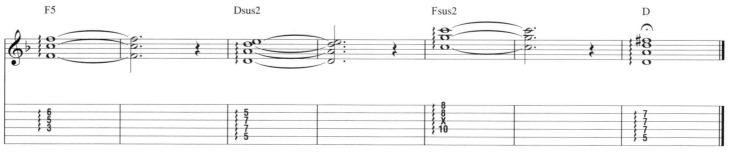

No Sunlight

Words and Music by Benjamin Gibbard and Christopher Walla

Verse

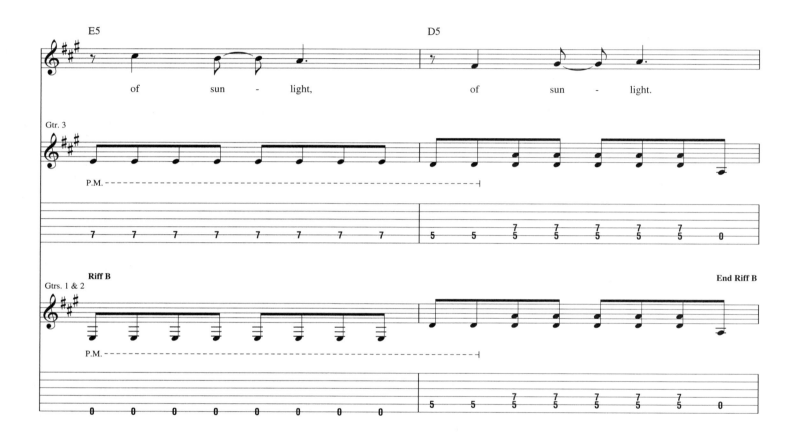

Chorus

No sun-light, no sun-light.

No sun-light, no sun-light.

28

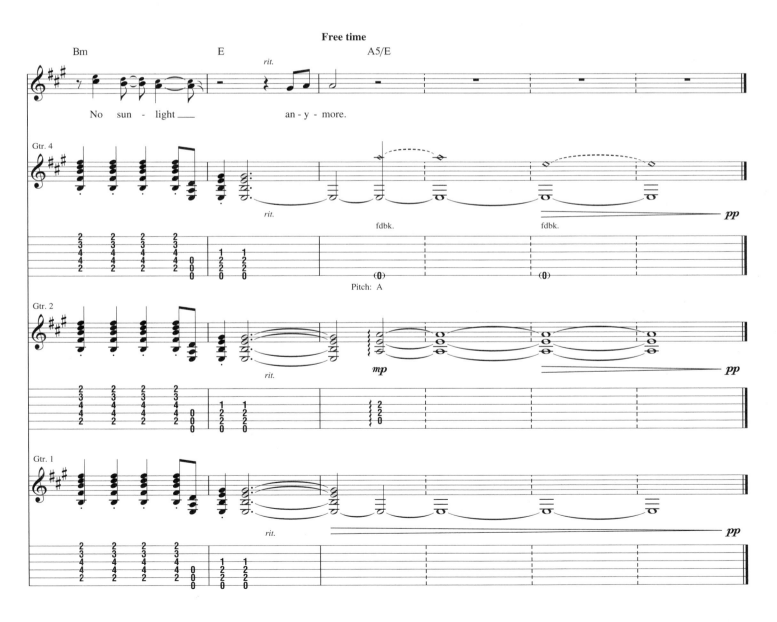

Cath

Words and Music by Benjamin Gibbard

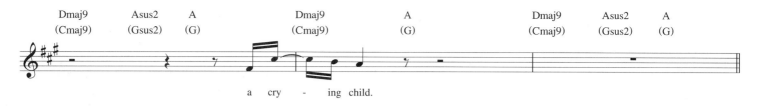

a cry - ing child.

% Chorus

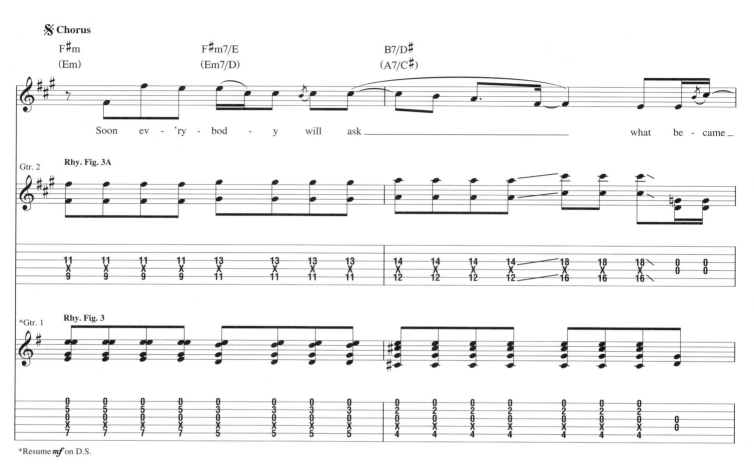

Soon ev - 'ry - bod – y will ask _____ what be - came _

Gtr. 2

Rhy. Fig. 3A

*Gtr. 1

Rhy. Fig. 3

*Resume *mf* on D.S.

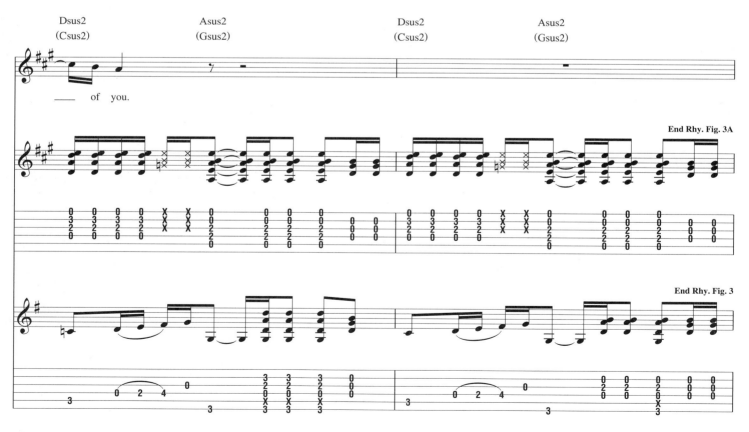

___ of you.

End Rhy. Fig. 3A

End Rhy. Fig. 3

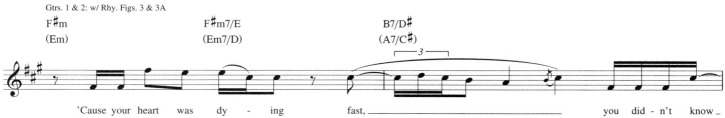

'Cause your heart was dy-ing fast,   you did-n't know

To Coda ⊕

what to do.

Interlude

Verse

2. Cath,   it seems   that you live   in some-one else's   dream

in a hand   me down   wed-ding dress   with the things

The whis-pers that it won't last _____ roll up and down ___ the pews.

But if their hearts were dy - ing that fast, _____ they'd have done the same ___ as you.

And I'd have done the same ___ as you.

Talking Bird

Words and Music by Benjamin Gibbard

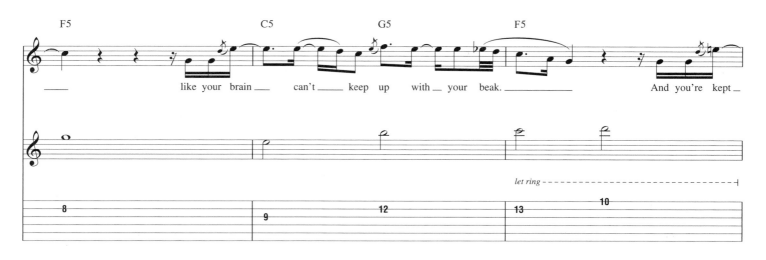

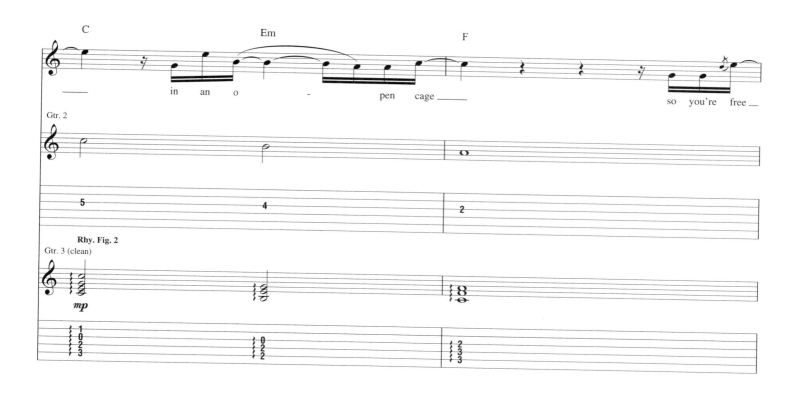

in an o - pen cage so you're free

Gtr. 2

Rhy. Fig. 2
Gtr. 3 (clean)
mp

to leave or stay. And some - times

End Rhy. Fig. 2

Gtr. 3: w/ Rhy. Fig. 2

you get con - fused, like there is a hint

Gtr. 2

that I'm _____ try - ing _____ to give you. _____ The

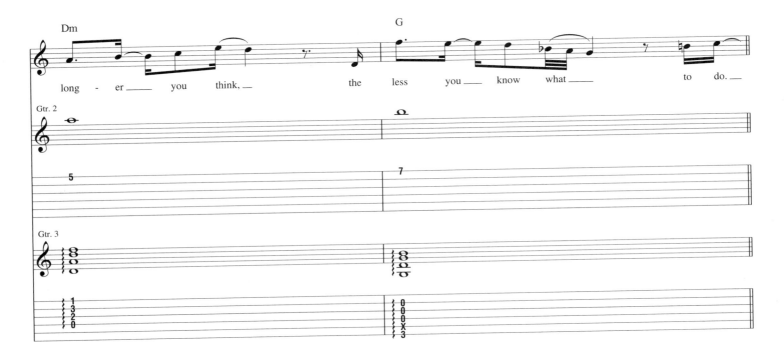

long - er _____ you think, _____ the less you _____ know what _____ to do. _____

Gtr. 2

Gtr. 3

Interlude

Gtr. 2 tacet
Gtr. 3: w/ Rhy. Fig. 2

2. It's hard _____

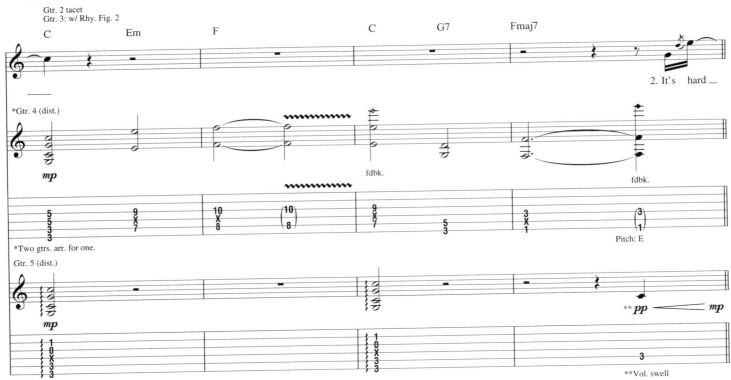

*Gtr. 4 (dist.)

*Two gtrs. arr. for one.

Gtr. 5 (dist.)

**Vol. swell

hey. ____ It's all here ___ for you ___ as

Free time

long as ___ you don't ___ fly a - way. ___

*Use vol. knob to create dynamic swells.

Pitch: E

You Can Do Better Than Me

Words and Music by Benjamin Gibbard

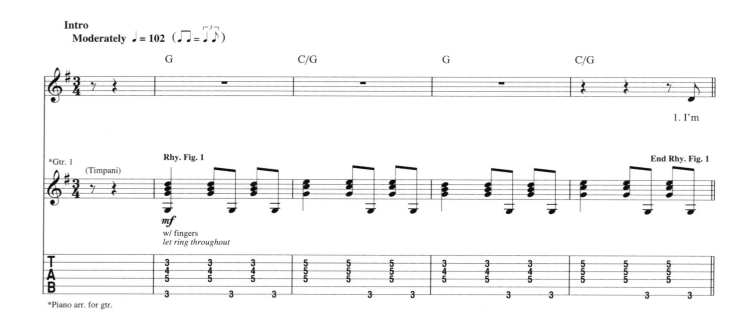

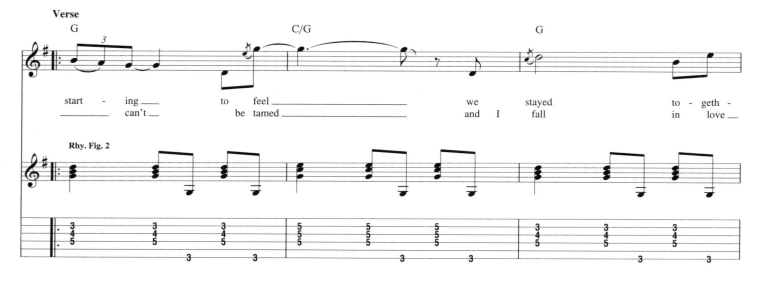

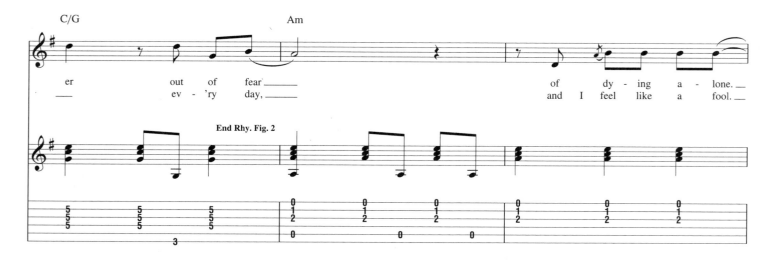

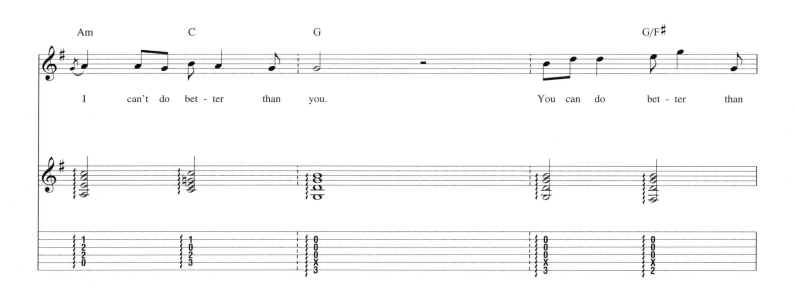

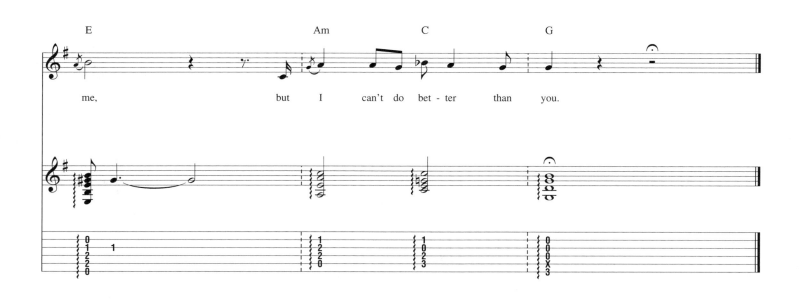

Grapevine Fires

Words and Music by Benjamin Gibbard, Jason McGerr and Nicholas Harmer

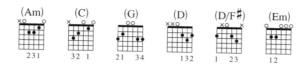

Capo III

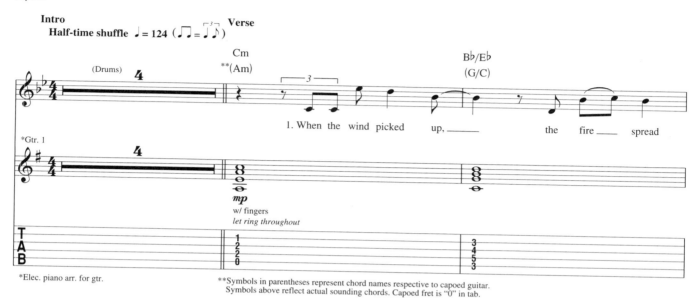

*Elec. piano arr. for gtr.

**Symbols in parentheses represent chord names respective to capoed guitar.
Symbols above reflect actual sounding chords. Capoed fret is "0" in tab.

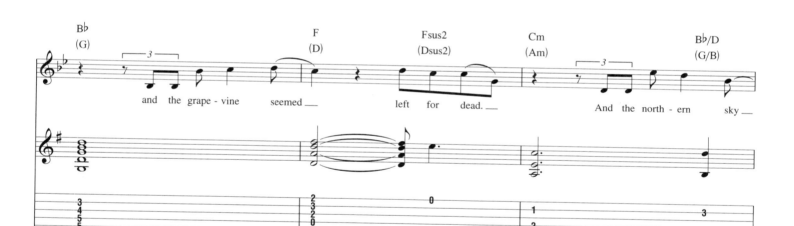

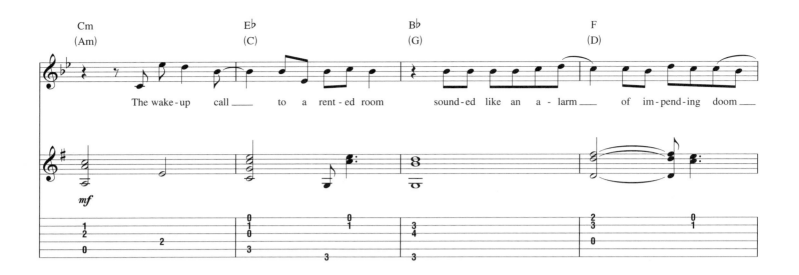

The wake-up call ___ to a rent-ed room sound-ed like an a-larm ___ of im-pend-ing doom ___

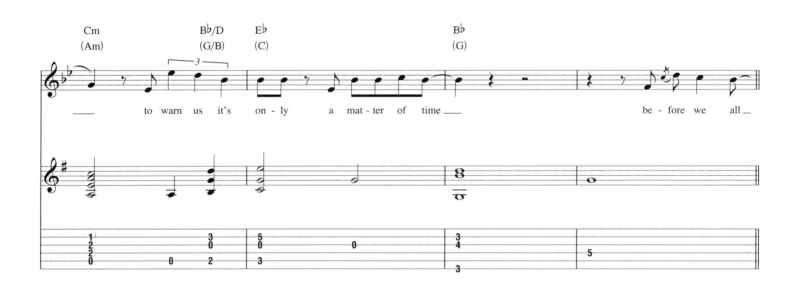

___ to warn us it's on-ly a mat-ter of time ___ be-fore we all ___

Chorus

Gtr. 1 tacet

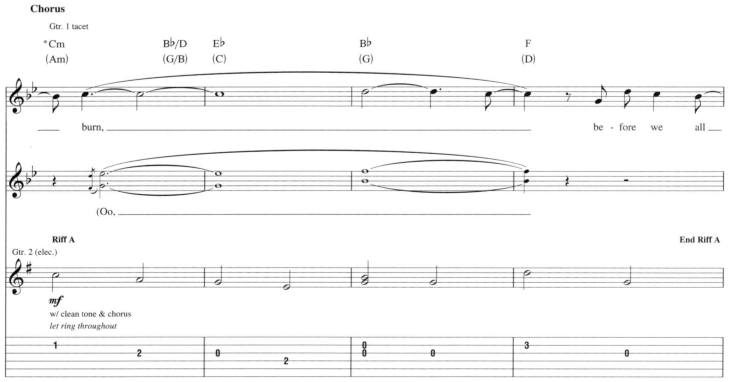

___ burn, _____ be-fore we all ___

(Oo, _____

Riff A

Gtr. 2 (elec.)

End Riff A

w/ clean tone & chorus
let ring throughout

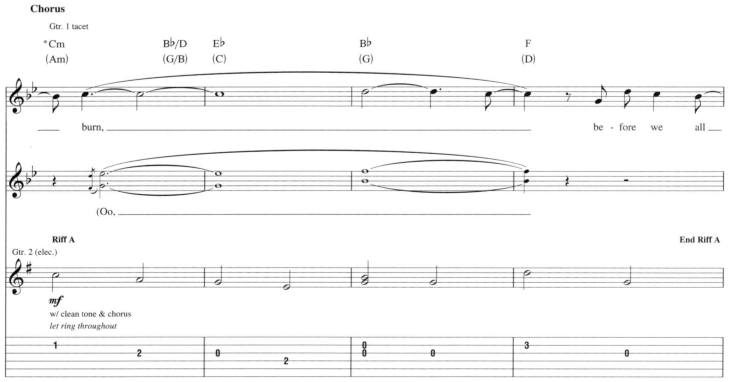

*Chord symbols reflect overall harmony.

Verse

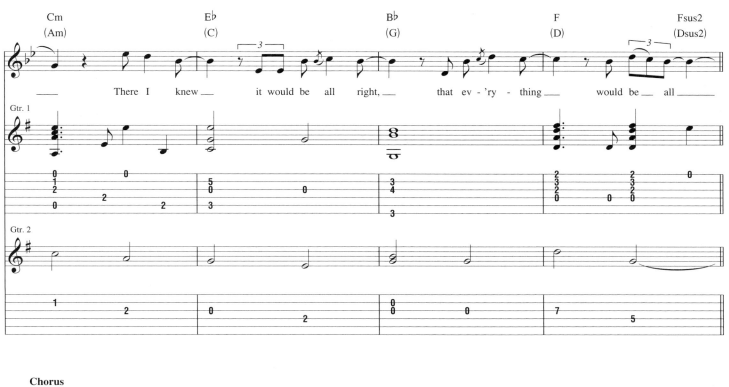

There I knew ____ it would be all right, ____ that ev-'ry-thing ____ would be ____ all

Chorus

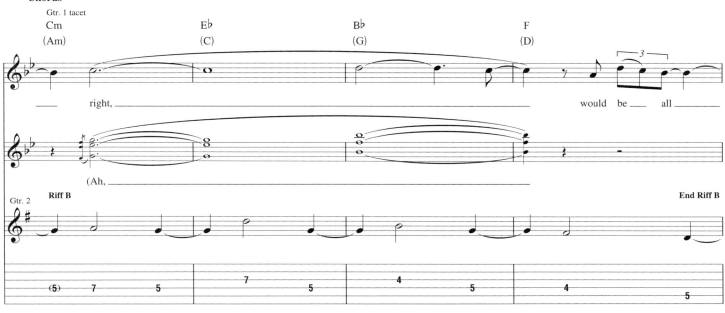

____ right, _____ would be ____ all ____

(Ah, _____

____ right, _____ would be ____ all _____

ah, _____

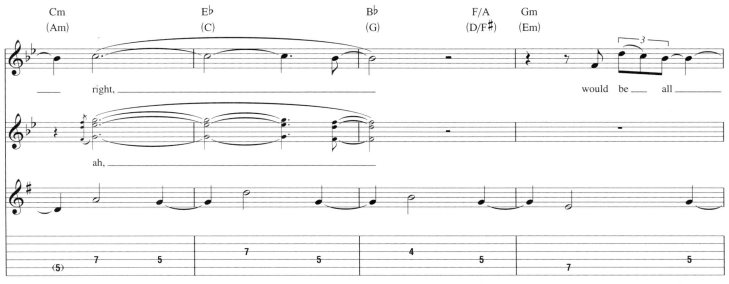

Gtr. 2: w/ Riff B

Cm (Am)   Eb (C)   Bb (G)   F (D)

right, _____ would be ___ all _____

ah.) _____

Cm (Am)   Eb (C)   Bb (G)

right. _____

Gtr. 2

Bridge

D7 (B7)   Eb/Bb (C/G)   Bb (G)

And the news re-ports _____ on the ra-di-o _____ said it was get-ting worse

Rhy. Fig. 1

*Gtrs. 2 & 3

*Gtr. 3 (acous.), doubled throughout, played *mp*.

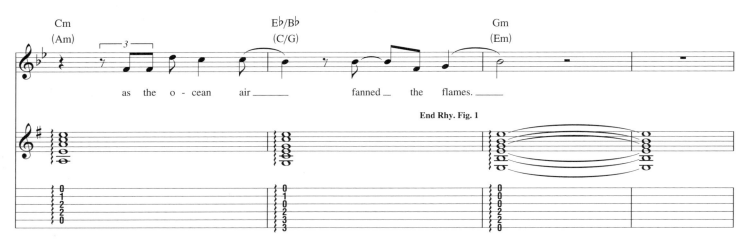

Cm (Am)   Eb/Bb (C/G)   Gm (Em)

as the o-cean air _____ fanned ___ the flames. _____

End Rhy. Fig. 1

Gtrs. 2 & 3: w/ Rhy. Fig. 1

But I could -n't think _____ of an - y - where _____ I would have rath -

er been to watch it all _____ burn _____ a - way, _____

to burn a - way. _____

Guitar Solo

Gtrs. 3 & 4 tacet

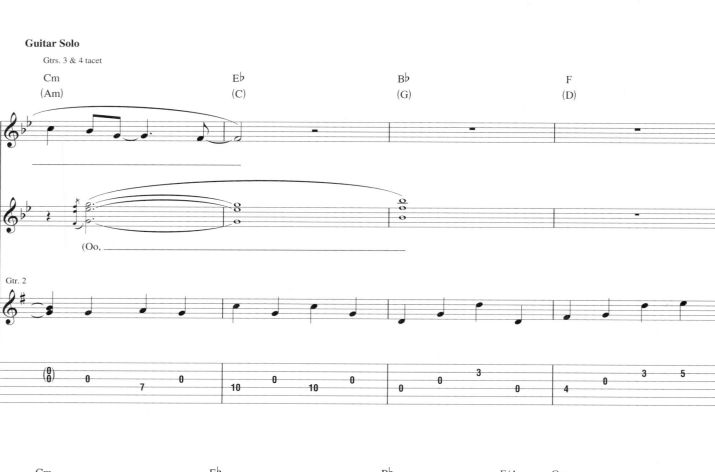

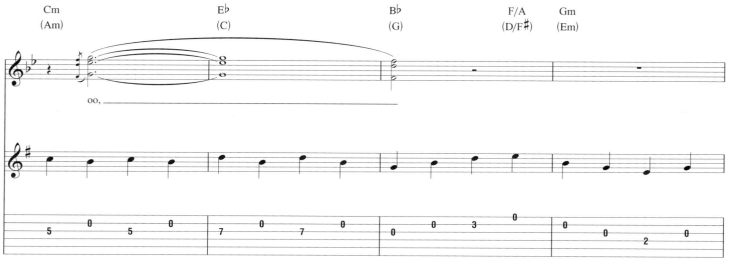

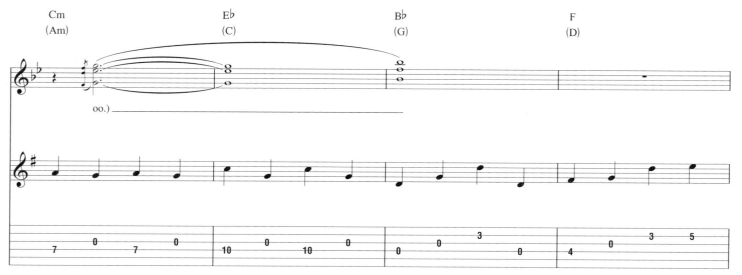

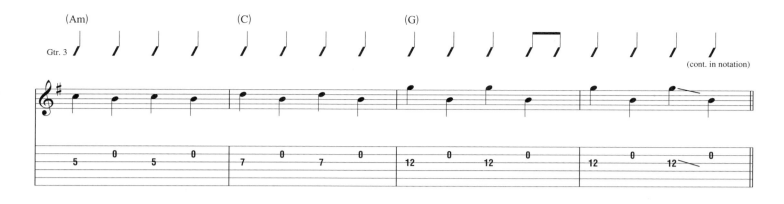

Outro

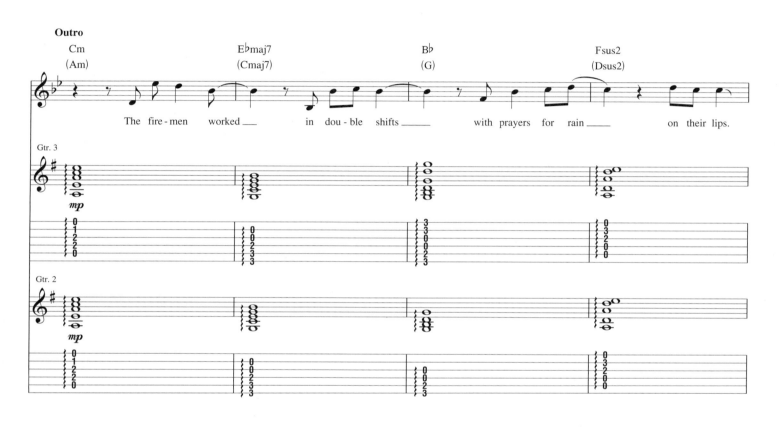

The fire-men worked ___ in dou-ble shifts ___ with prayers for rain ___ on their lips.

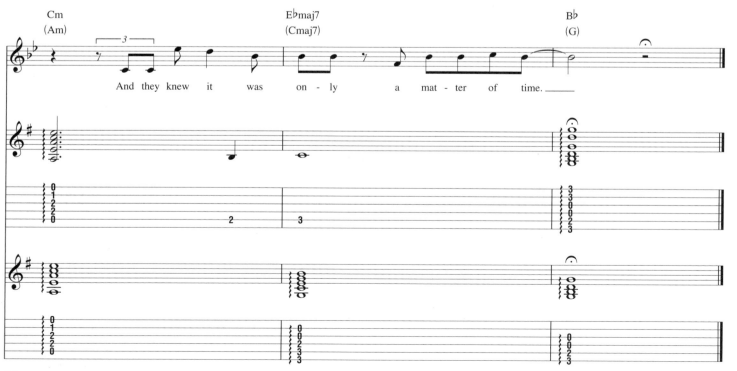

And they knew it was on-ly a mat-ter of time. ___

Your New Twin Sized Bed

Words and Music by Benjamin Gibbard and Nicholas Harmer

Gtrs. 2 & 3: Capo I

Intro

Moderately slow ♩ = 85

*Chord symbols reflect implied harmony.

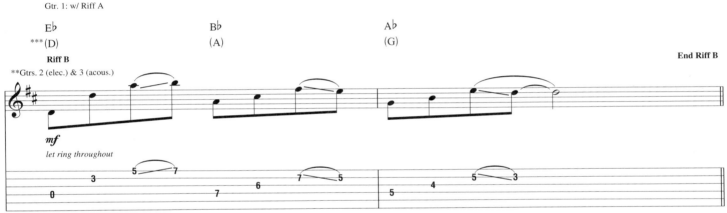

**Gtr. 2 w/ clean tone.

***Symbols in parentheses represent chord names respective to capoed guitars.
Symbols above reflect actual sounding chords. Capoed fret is "0" in tab.

Verse

1st time, Gtr. 1: w/ Riff A
Gtrs. 2 & 3 tacet
2nd time, Gtr. 1: w/ Riff D

1. You look so de-feat-ed ly-ing there ___ in your new twin sized ___ bed, ___
2. You used ___ to think ___ that ___ some-one ___ would come a - long

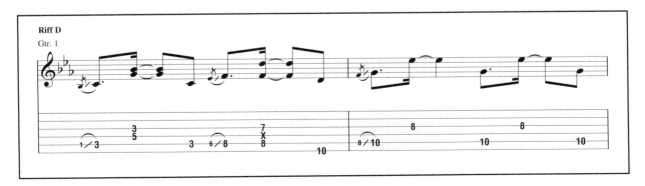

with a sin - gle pil - low un - der - neath _____ your sin - gle ____ head.
and lay ____ be - side ____ you ____ in the space that they be - long.

But the

I guess you de - cid - ed that that old queen _____ was more space ____ than you ____ would need. ____
oth - er side of the mat - tress and box ____ spring ____ stayed ____ like ____ new.

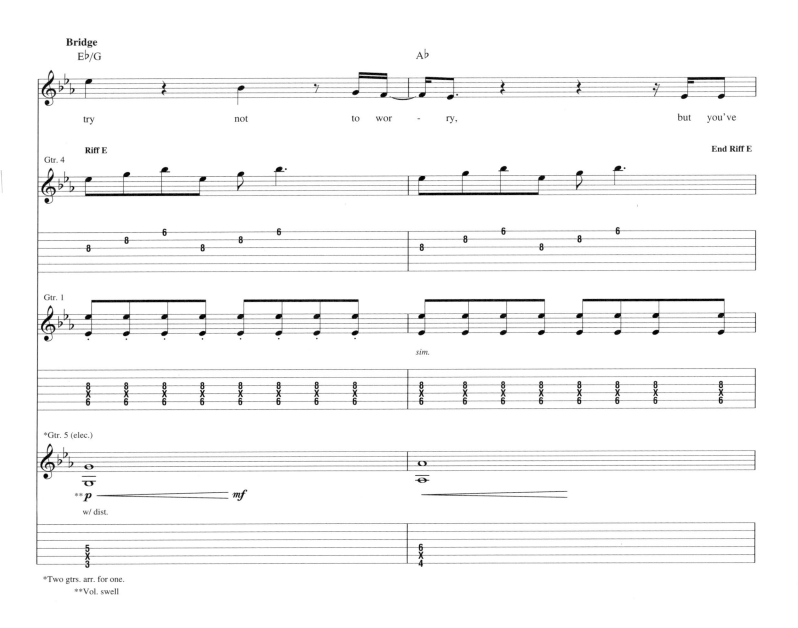

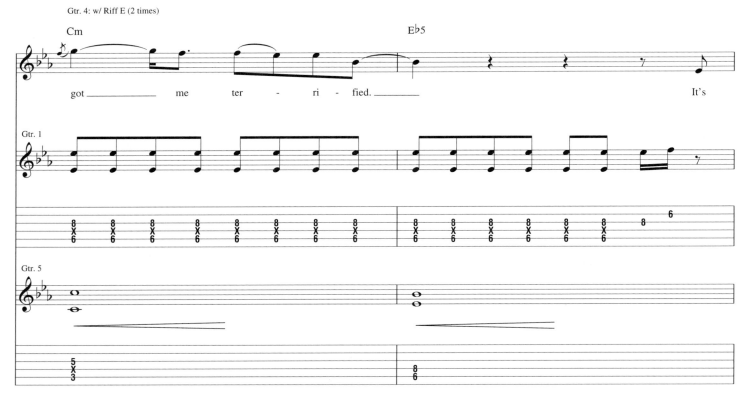

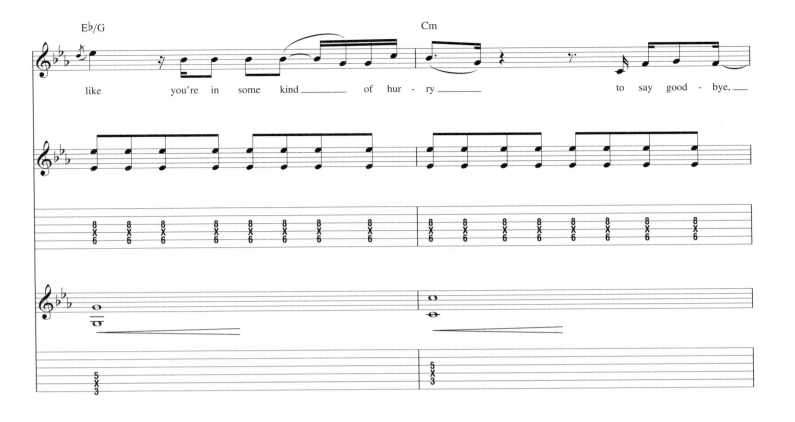

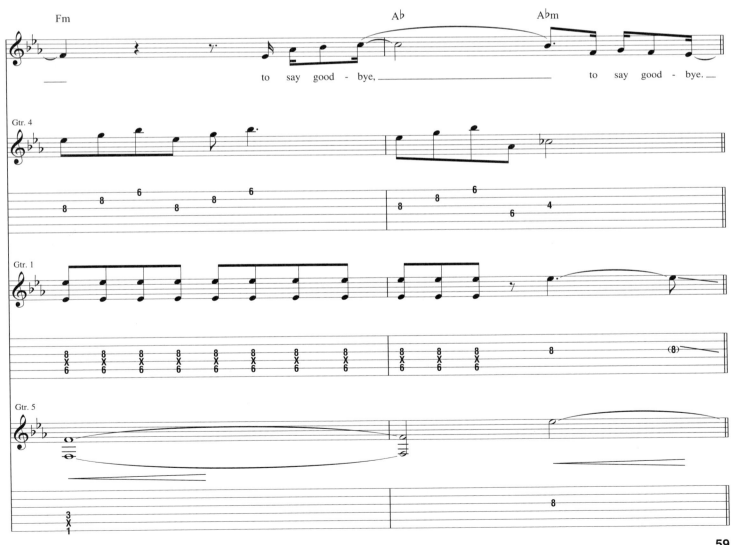

Interlude

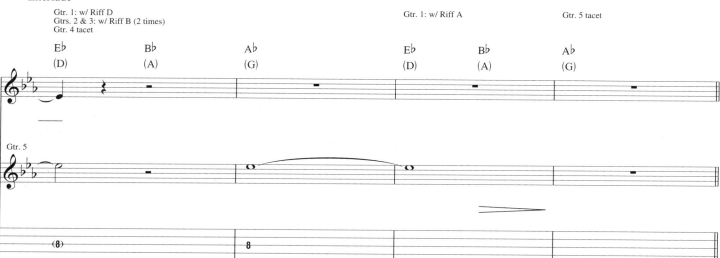

Outro

You look so de-feat - ed ly - ing there ___ in your new twin sized ___ bed. ___

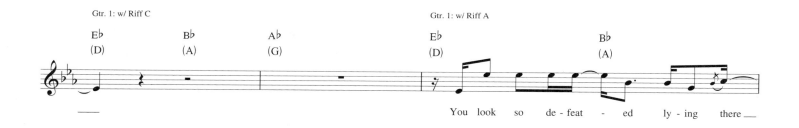

___ You look so de-feat - ed ly - ing there ___

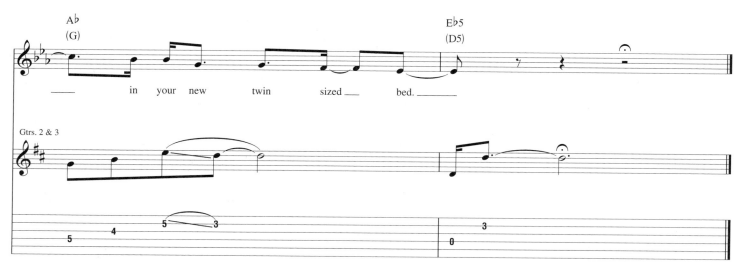

___ in your new twin sized ___ bed. _____

Long Division

Words and Music by Benjamin Gibbard, Nicholas Harmer and Christopher Walla

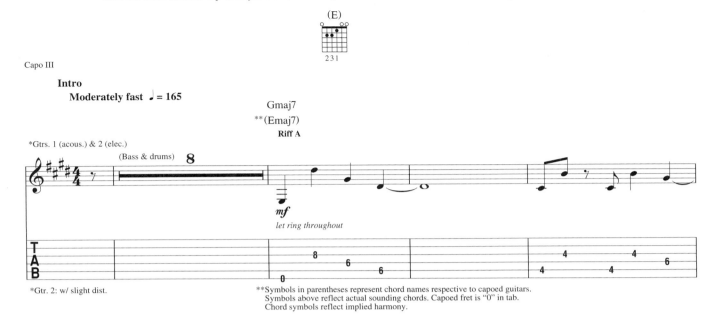

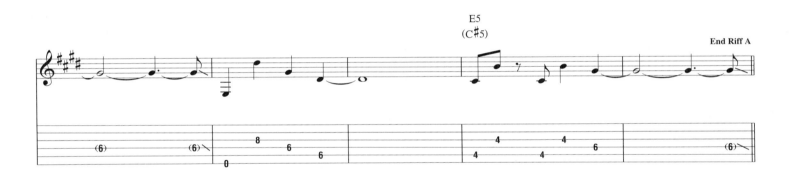

Verse

Gtr. 1: w/ Riff A (2 times)
Gtr. 2: w/ Riff A (1 1/2 times)

1. His head was a cit-y of pa-per build-ings

and the ech-oes that ___ re-mained ___

of old friends and lov-ers, their fea-tures bleed-ing

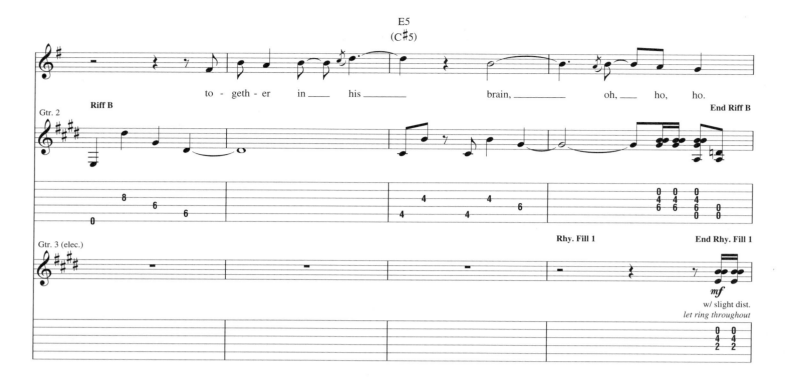

E5
(C#5)

to - geth - er in ___ his ___ brain, ___ oh, ___ ho, ho.

Gtr. 2   Riff B   End Riff B

Gtr. 3 (elec.)   Rhy. Fill 1   End Rhy. Fill 1

mf
w/ slight dist.
let ring throughout

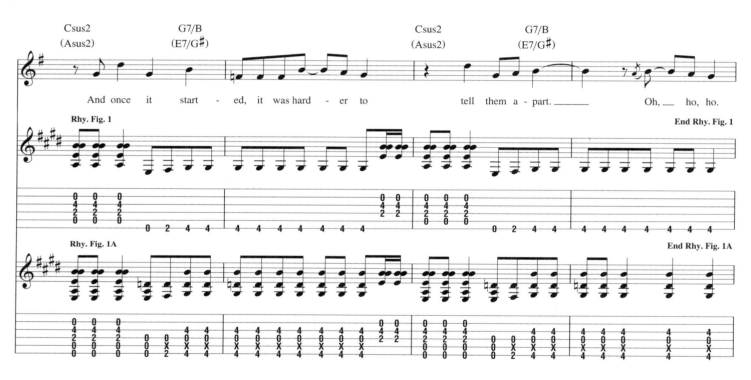

Csus2   G7/B   Csus2   G7/B
(Asus2)   (E7/G#)   (Asus2)   (E7/G#)

And once it start - ed, it was hard - er to ___ tell them a - part. ___ Oh, ___ ho, ho.

Rhy. Fig. 1   End Rhy. Fig. 1

Rhy. Fig. 1A   End Rhy. Fig. 1A

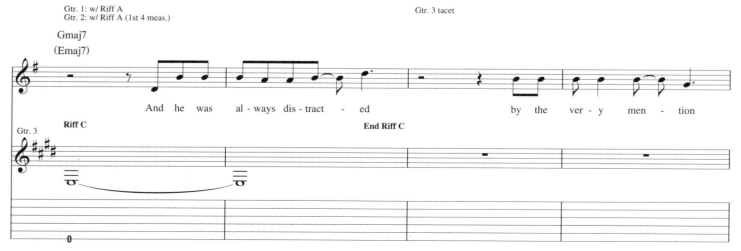

Gtr. 1: w/ Riff A
Gtr. 2: w/ Riff A (1st 4 meas.)   Gtr. 3 tacet

Gmaj7
(Emaj7)

And he was al - ways dis - tract - ed ___ by the ver - y men - tion

Gtr. 3   Riff C   End Riff C

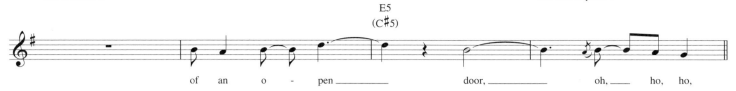

of an o - pen ____ door, ____ oh, ____ ho, ho,

Pre-Chorus

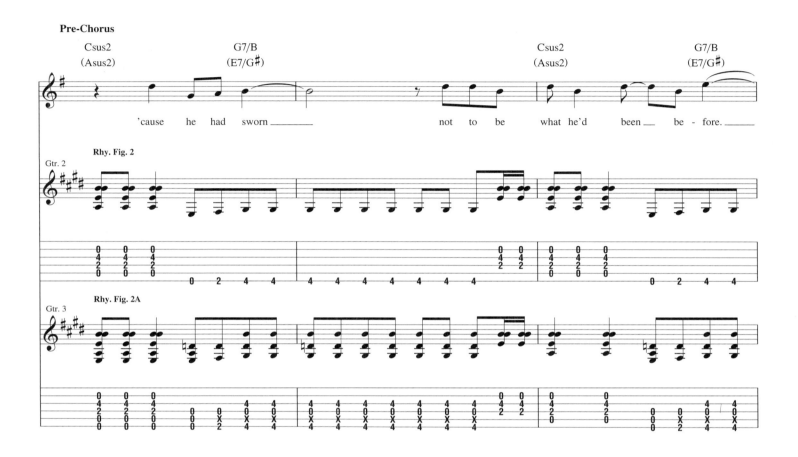

'cause he had sworn ____ not to be what he'd been __ be - fore. ____

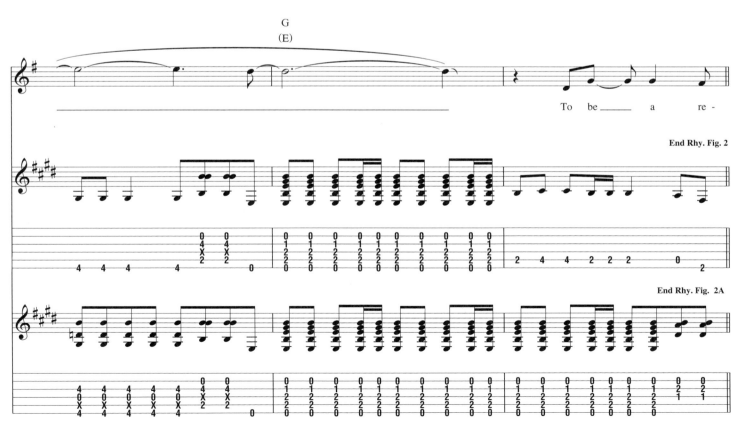

To be ____ a re -

Chorus

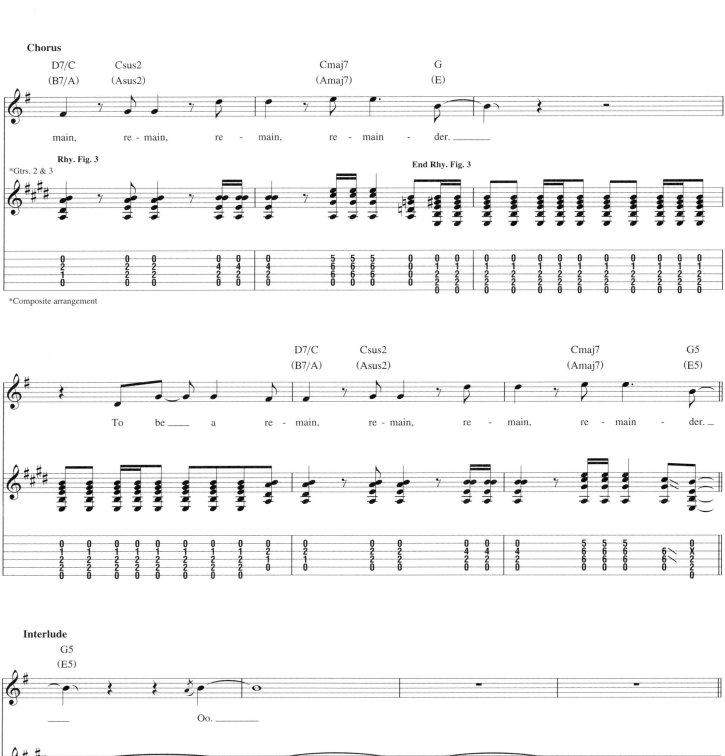

main, re - main, re - main, re - main - der.

*Gtrs. 2 & 3

*Composite arrangement

To be a re - main, re - main, re - main, re - main - der.

Interlude

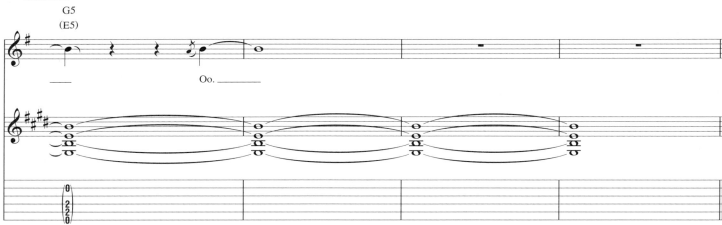

Oo.

Verse

Gtr. 1: w/ Riff A (2 times)
Gtr. 2: w/ Riff A (1 1/2 times)
Gtr. 3 tacet

2. The tel - e - vi - sion was snow - ing soft - ly

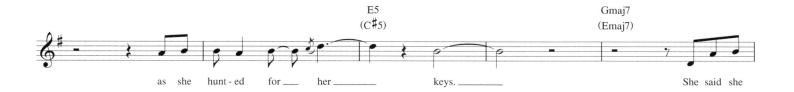

as she hunt-ed for __ her __ keys. ____ She said she

Gtr. 2: w/ Riff B

nev-er en-vi-sioned him the type of per-son . ca-pa-

Gtr. 3: w/ Rhy. Fill 1   Gtrs. 2 & 3: w/ Rhy. Figs. 1 & 1A

ble __ of such __ de-ceit, ____ oh, __ ho, ho. Oh, __ ho, ho. __

Gtr. 1: w/ Riff A
Gtr. 2: w/ Riff A (1st 4 meas.)
Gtr. 3: w/ Riff C

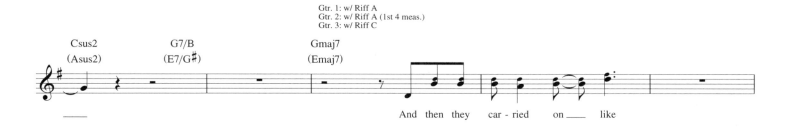

____ And then they car-ried on __ like

Gtr. 2: w/ Riff B   Gtr. 3: w/ Rhy. Fill 1

long di-vi-sion, as it was clear with ev-'ry ____ page, ____ oh, __ that they

Pre-Chorus

Gtrs. 2 & 3: w/ Rhy. Figs. 2 & 2A

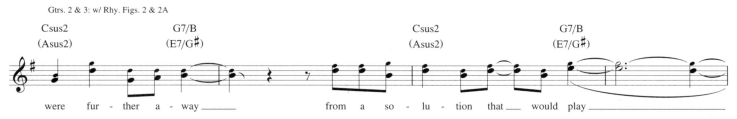

were fur-ther a-way ____ from a so-lu-tion that __ would play ____

𝄉 **Chorus**

Gtrs. 2 & 3: w/ Rhy. Fig. 3

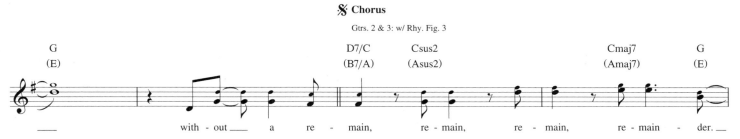

____ with-out __ a re-main, re-main, re-main, re-main-der. __

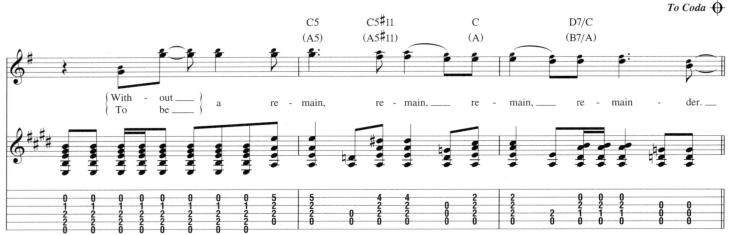

Guitar Solo

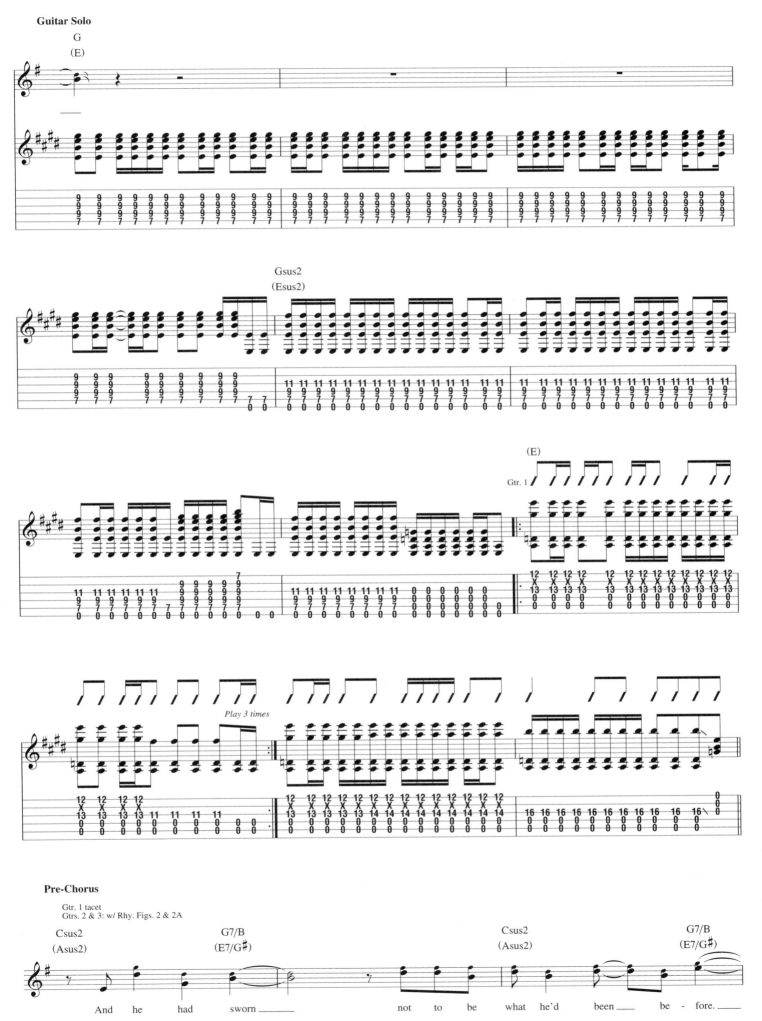

Pre-Chorus

Gtr. 1 tacet
Gtrs. 2 & 3: w/ Rhy. Figs. 2 & 2A

And he had sworn _____ not to be what he'd been _____ be - fore. _____

Coda

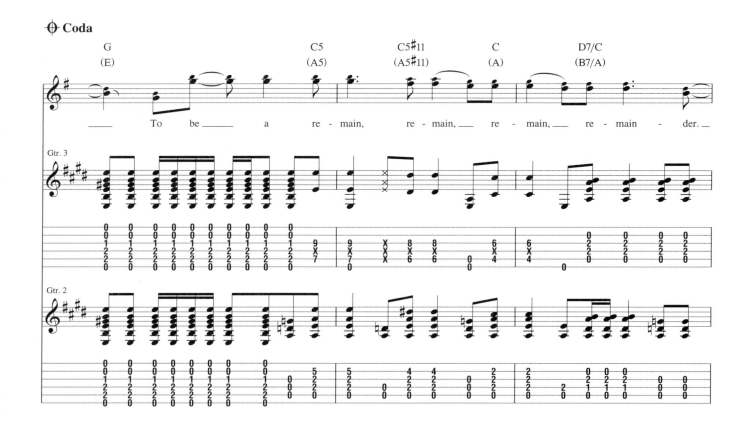

To be ___ a re - main, re - main, ___ re - main, ___ re - main - der. ___

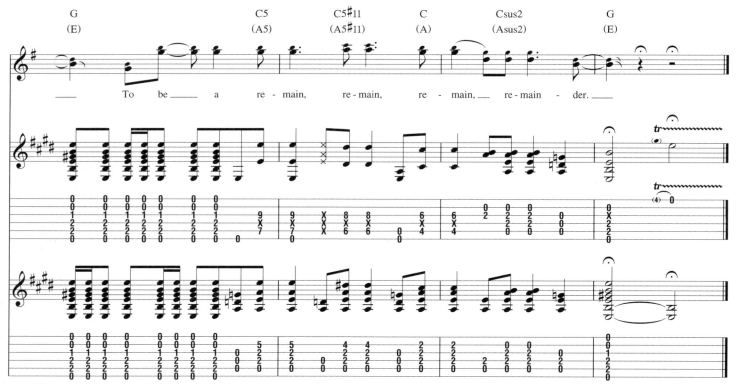

To be ___ a re - main, re - main, re - main, ___ re - main - der. ___

Pity and Fear

Words and Music by Benjamin Gibbard

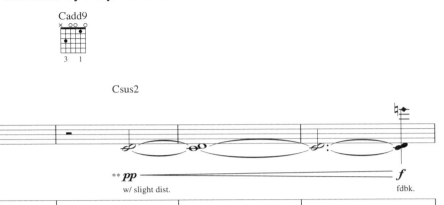

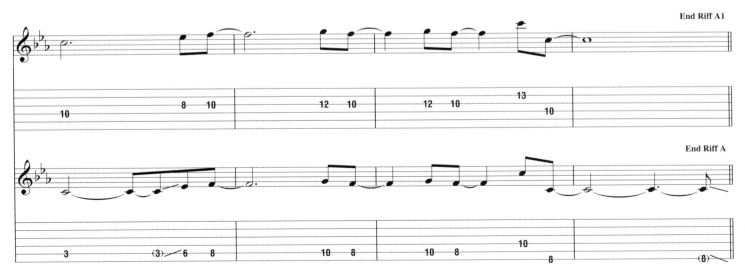

%% **Verse**

Gtrs. 2 & 3: w/ Riffs A & A1 (2 times)
2nd time, Gtr. 1 tacet

1. I have ___ such en - vy ___ for the stran - ger ly - ing
2. A storm ___ at sea, ___ the bow cracked ___ and I was

next to me who a - wakes ___ in the night ___
cap - siz - ing. And I sunk ___ be - low, ___

and slips out ___ in - to the pre - dawn light with no words, ___
where I swore ___ I would nev - er go. If you can't ___

a clean es - cape, ___ no prom - is - es or mess - es made, and
stand in place, ___ you can't ___ tell who's walk - ing a - way from

To Coda ⊕

chalks it all up ___ to mis - take, ___ mis - take, ___ mis - take. ___ } And
who re - mains, ___ who stays, ___ who stays, ___ who stays. ___ }

Chorus

Cadd9

Rhy. Fig. 1

Gtr. 4
(acous.)
pp

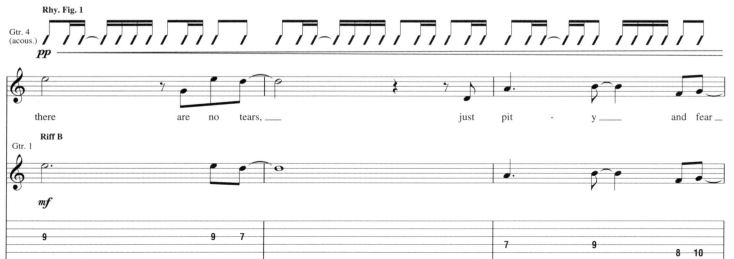

there are no tears, ___ just pit - y ___ and fear ___

Riff B
Gtr. 1
mf

70

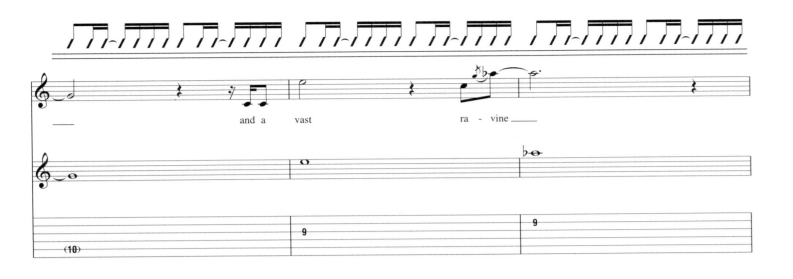

and a vast   ra - vine

Interlude

Cadd9

End Rhy. Fig. 1

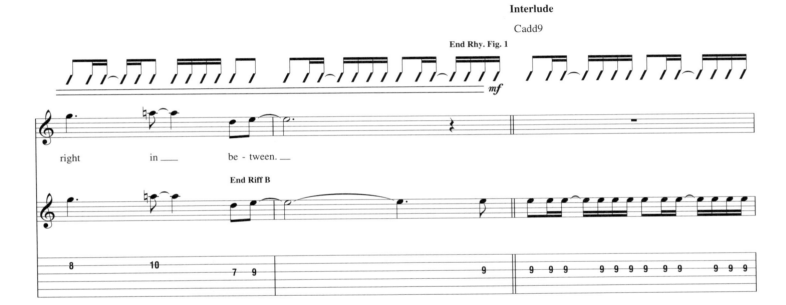

mf

right   in ___ be - tween. ___

End Riff B

D.S. al Coda

⊕ Coda

Chorus

Gtr. 1: w/ Riff B
*Gtr. 4: w/ Rhy. Fig. 1 (2 times)

Cadd9

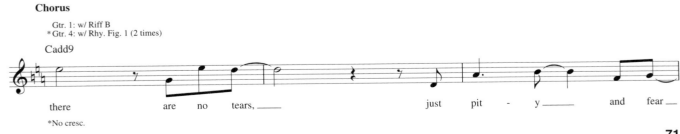

there   are   no   tears, ___   just   pit - y ___   and   fear

*No cresc.

and a vast ra - vine _____ right in _____ be - tween.

Gtr. 1: w/ Fill 1   Gtr. 1: w/ Riff B

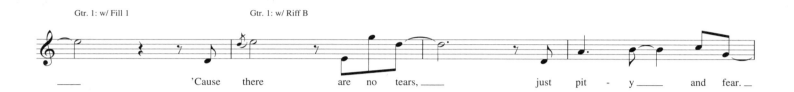

_____ 'Cause there are no tears, _____ just pit - y _____ and fear.

_____ And I re - call _____ the push more _____ than the fall,

Gtr. 4: w/ Rhy. Fig. 1 (last 2 meas.)

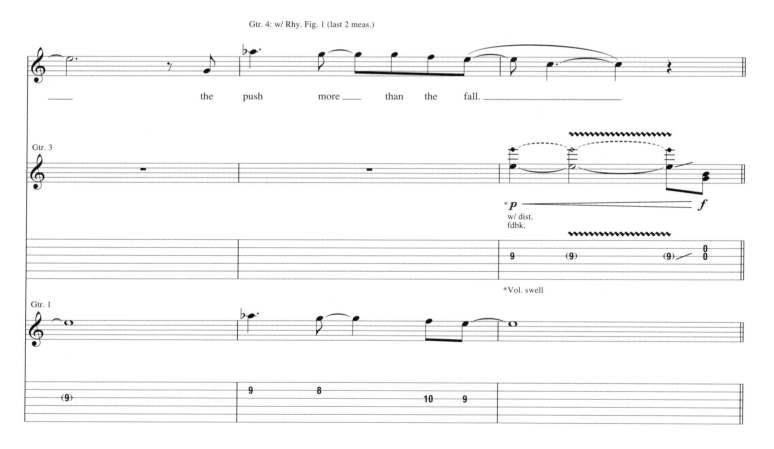

the push more _____ than the fall. _____

Gtr. 3

*p _____ f
w/ dist.
fdbk.

*Vol. swell

Gtr. 1

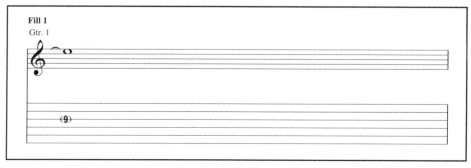

Fill 1
Gtr. 1

72

Outro

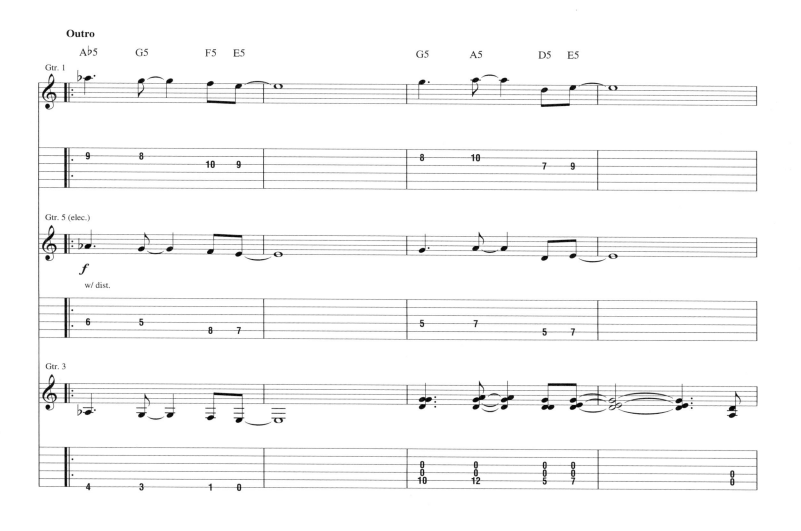

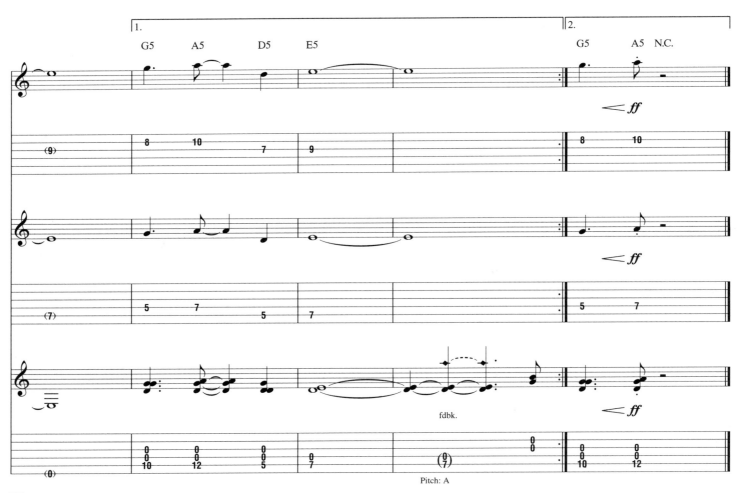

Pitch: A

The Ice Is Getting Thinner

Words and Music by Benjamin Gibbard and Christopher Walla

Drop D tuning:
(low to high) D-A-D-G-B-E

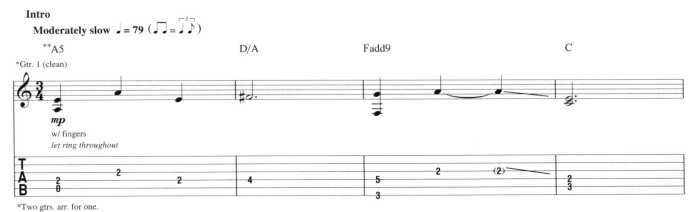

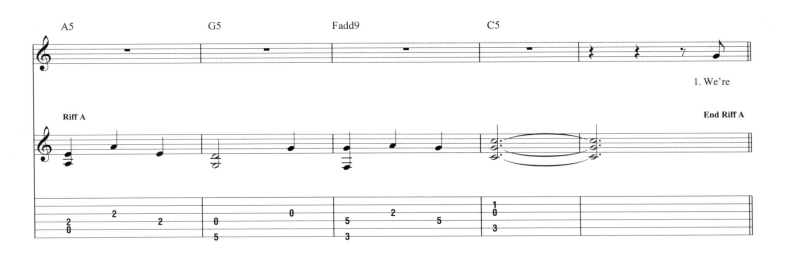

and so have we. ____ There was lit- tle we ___ could say ___

Gtr. 1: w/ Riff A

and e - ven less ___ that we could do ___ to stop the ice from get - ting thin -

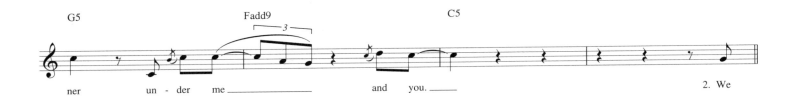

ner un - der me ____ and you. ____

2. We

Verse

Gtr. 1: w/ Riff C

bur-ied our love ____ in a win - ter - y ___ grave. ____

A

76

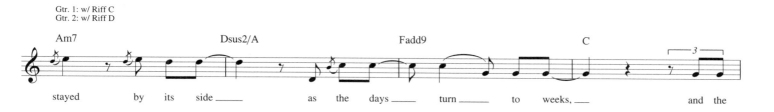

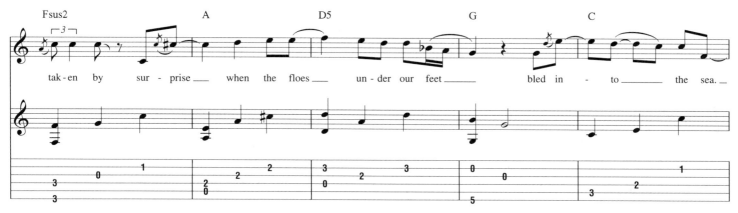

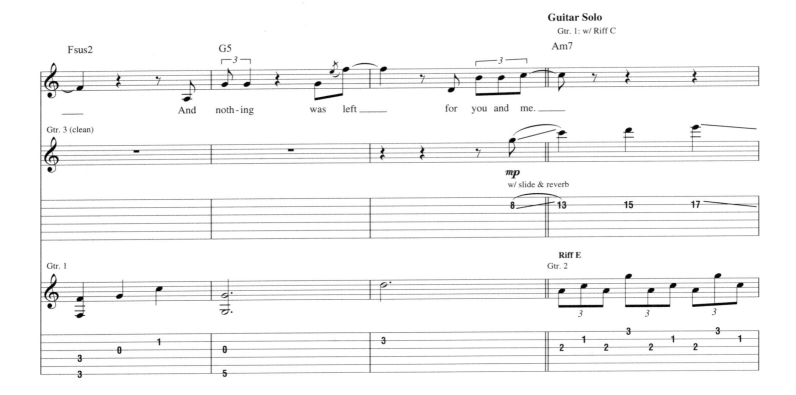

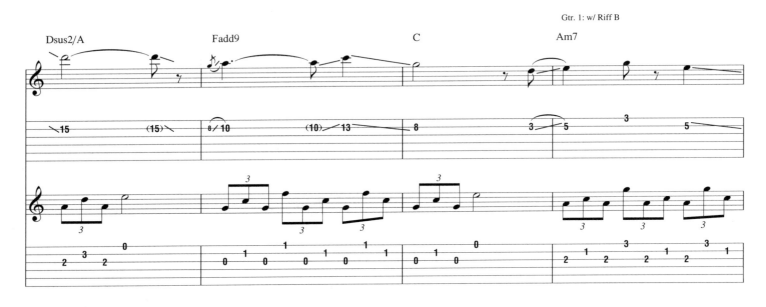

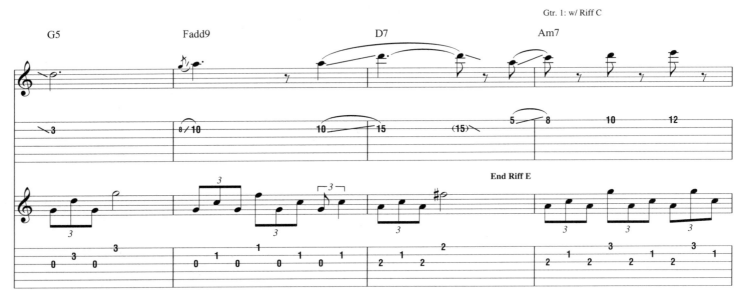

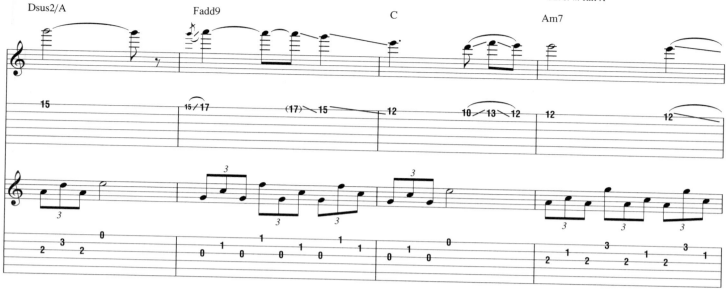

Gtr. 1: w/ Riff B

Am7   G5   Fadd9   D7

no - where we can go   with noth - ing un - der - neath.   And it

Gtr. 1: w/ Riff C

Am7   Dsus2/A   Fadd9   C

sad - dens me __ to say ___ what we both __ knew was __ true, ___ that the

1.

Am7   G5   Fadd9

ice was get - ting thin - ner un - der me ___ and you. __

Gtr. 2

Gtr. 1

2.

C   Fsus2   C5

The ___ and you. ___

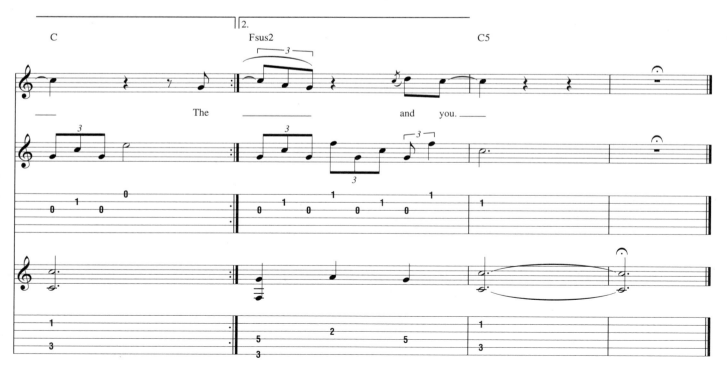